An Alphabetical Walk . . .
. . . around your body

Take an imaginary walk around your body. Look for parts that begin with various letters of the alphabet. Can you find at least one part for each letter of the alphabet? Print the letter where the part is located. On this page list the various parts you find that begin with each letter.

A. _____

B. _____

C. _____

D. _____

E. _____

F. _____

G. _____

H. _____

I. _____

J-K. _____

L. _____

M. _____

N. _____

O._____ P. _____

Q._____

S. _____

T._____ U-V.___ _____

W. _____

X-Y-Z. _____

Hey, What's Up?

What would be different for us and our bodies if all of a sudden we walked on our hands instead of our feet?

How would people's lives change?

Body Adaptations

_____
_____
_____
_____
_____
_____
_____
_____
_____
_____
_____
_____
_____
_____
_____
_____
_____
_____
_____
_____
_____
_____
_____
_____

At Home

_____
_____
_____
_____
_____
_____

At School

_____
_____
_____
_____
_____

In Sports

_____
_____
_____
_____

At Work

_____
_____
_____
_____

GGA113
Copyright © 1997 Gary Grimm & Associates

-Dentification

Our eyes are our most important sense organs. The eye can provide us with great detail.

Creating an "Eye" D of Your Eyes

The shape: _____ The size: _____
The colors: _____
Other characteristics: _____
_____
Three protectors of my eyes are _____
_____, and _____,
_____.

Sometimes "EYES" have some problems and/or diseases like not being able to read or not being able to see objects in the distance. "Eye" bet that you know some of my problems. Can you name some eye problems that you, your family, or friends have or have had?

_____   _____   _____
_____   _____   _____

My cornea can be transplanted. This allows people who are losing or who have lost their sight to see. List below some things you would miss seeing the most if you were to lose your sight.

_____
_____
_____
_____
_____
_____
_____
_____
_____

The Eye

Study the illustration above. Can you identify each part of the eye?

☐ iris   ☐ pupil
☐ cornea   ☐ lens
☐ retina   ☐ optic nerve

Copyright © 1997 Gary Grimm & Associates

Body Parts — Transplants

George Washington, the "Father of Our Country," had a set of false teeth. We have all read about pirates with wooden legs or hooks for arms. Medical science has progressed quite far since those primitive replacement parts were used. Today just about everything in the body can be replaced by man-made devices (knee and hip joints) or through donor transplants (hearts, kidneys). Scientists, doctors, and technologists continue to work, to discover, to invent. Someday we might be able to regenerate (regrow) our own body parts. When a starfish loses one of its arms, it grows back. While we might not always agree which organs should be donated/transplanted or how much the body should be re-created with artificial implants, technology continues; experimentation goes on.

CORNEAS   KIDNEYS   HEARTS   LIVERS

Besides the heart and kidneys, what other organs can be donated and transplanted?

_____
_____
_____

Would you be a donor? Why? Why not?

_____
_____
_____
_____

Would you accept someone's donation – a heart, an eye, a kidney? Why? Why not?

_____
_____
_____
_____
_____

What do you think the future holds in store for man as far as transplants are concerned?

_____
_____
_____
_____

Besides knee and hip joints, what other man-made devices are available?

_____
_____
_____

What man-made devices will be available in the future?

_____
_____
_____

Copyright © 1997 Gary Grimm & Associates

Who Are You?
Just Ask Your Brain

It is odd, but when we think that we love someone, we think it is our heart that is involved. Thoughts that make us cry, smile, or become angry, as well as loving feelings, come straight from the brain. In addition to emotions, all of our thinking abilities and "directions" for our bodily functions come from the brain.

Suppose brains could be transplanted and that someone gets YOUR brain. Would that person become YOU?

_____

_____

_____

What if YOUR brain was placed in an older person's body? What might some of the consequences be?

_____

_____

_____

What if you received the brain of someone of the opposite sex. How would that affect you?

_____

_____

_____

What would your brain bring to a different body concerning . . .

Hobbies: _____

Fears: _____

Friends: _____

Intelligence: _____

Childhood Memories: _____

Bad Habits: _____

Good Habits: _____

It might be difficult to know just who YOU were because _____

_____

Copyright © 1997 Gary Grimm & Associates

Designer "Genes"

If scientific technology continues to expand in the future, you just might be able to choose many of the traits and characteristics of your children.

There are forty-eight chromosomes (twenty-four from each parent). The genes (X, Y) on each chromosome have been identified, so scientists know which gene is predicting hair and eye color, etc.

The genes also tell us if we might be candidates for certain diseases, like cancer, or even if we might be bald. Each parent would have to supply a similar gene for a trait to appear.

This causes some interesting questions to arise as well as some potential problems.

If you were a parent and could choose "traits" for your children before they were born, which ones might you and your spouse want to choose and what might your choices be?

height _____

weight _____

eye color _____

hair color _____

I.Q. _____

athletic ability _____

musical talent _____

double jointedness _____

Other traits that you think are important to consider:

_____

_____

_____

_____

Think of some of the problems that could exist if parents chose their children's traits.

For the Child _____

_____

_____

_____

For the Parents _____

_____

_____

_____

For the School _____

_____

_____

_____

For Society _____

_____

_____

_____

Don't Be "Alarmed" by This Fire!

"A fire! Run! Get help! Call the fire department!" This would be a typical response in an emergency. But fire has an interesting side too.

It's beautiful.

Its colors can be _____.

It has different movements: _____.

It's efficient.

It cleans nature's "house" by _____.

It doesn't leave "leftovers" because _____.

It's worth listening to as it consumes different materials.

When a pile of leaves is burning, it sounds like _____.

When cardboard boxes are burning, it sounds like _____.

When dry logs are burning in the fireplace, it sounds like _____.

Another good fire sound is when _____.

These sounds are probably caused by _____.

It's a sensation of smells.

What's the first word that comes to your mind with these things that involve burning or scorching?

Roasted marshmallows _____   Singed (burnt) hair _____

Burning rubber tires _____   Lighted scented candles _____

It's helpful.

List some ways we use fire to our advantage.

_____

_____

It's puzzling.

Its ashes weigh a lot. Why? _____

It can be started many ways without using a match. Name some. _____

_____

_____

_____

 Copyright © 1997 Gary Grimm & Associates

BONES

There are 206 bones in the human body. Can you name them? Just joking. However, below you will find a few listed. Draw an arrow from each word to its proper location. Maybe you could add a few more but only important ones, please. Okay, they are all important. So add a few of the more common ones.

skull

cranium

rib cage

spine

scapula

mandible

humerus

radius

pelvis

ulna

patella

femur

fibula

tibia

vertebrae

phalanges

Copyright © 1997 Gary Grimm & Associates

Eyes, Ears, Nose, Mouth

Does the word relate to your eye, your ear, your nose, or your mouth? Place each word found in the Word Bank below under the picture of the appropriate body part.

Word Bank

nostril
dentist
pupil
hearing
telephone
lashes
gums
cochlea
hammer
aroma

mucus
deafness
wax
focus
vibrations
cornea
taste
anvil
bridge
braille

roof
palate
retina
sty
sinus
visual
glaucoma
sight
saliva
sighing

smell
taste buds
uvula
audio
iris
tears
sound
lips
camera
tonsils

speech
gingivitis
optometrist
equilibrium
orthodontist
ophthalmologist
eustachian tube
astigmatism
balance

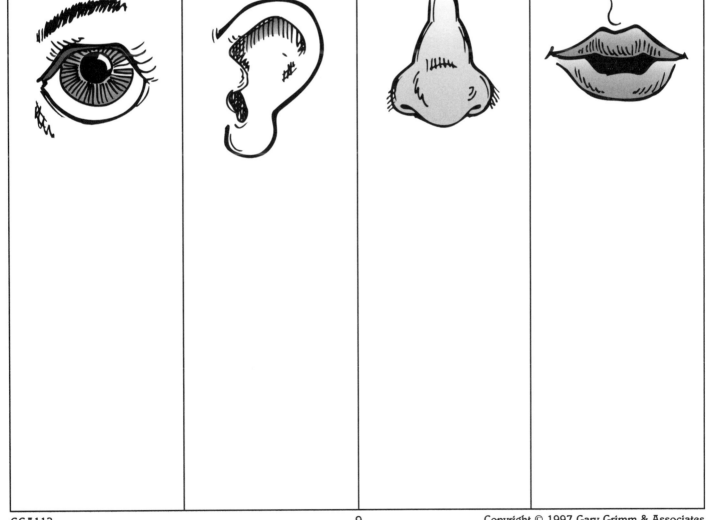

9 Copyright © 1997 Gary Grimm & Associates

Every Breath You Take

RELAX! Take a couple of deep breaths to help you relax. Let your mind wander a little. Just relax and BREATHE NORMALLY.

How many times do you breathe a minute? _____

First minute _____

Rest a minute

Second minute _____

Rest a minute

Third minute _____

Do you breathe the same number of times each minute? What is the average? Do you breathe through your nose, your mouth or through both at the same times? Try each method. Are the same number of breaths taken?

Breathing one minute by nose = _____ breaths.

Breathing one minute by mouth = _____ breaths.

Breathing one minute by both = _____ breaths.

Now that's a lot of AIR!

How many breaths would a typical person take in:

an hour _____   a month _____

a day _____   a year _____

a week _____   a lifetime _____

Copyright © 1997 Gary Grimm & Associates

Apartment Wanted

Pretend you are an owl whose home has been destroyed by a forest fire. You need to find a new place to live. Write a want ad for a newspaper requesting a new home. Be sure to include some details about what is required.

TreeTop Times
NATIONAL EDITION

Sunny
High 67 – Low 50's

Tuesday, April 12, 1999

_____
_____
_____
_____
_____
_____
_____
_____
_____
_____
_____
_____
_____
_____

I'm homeless. Please help me!

Some say that a forest fire is one way that Mother Nature cleans house. How does a forest fire clean house?

_____
_____
_____

Besides birds of all kinds, who is affected by a forest fire?

_____
_____
_____

11

Copyright © 1997 Gary Grimm & Associates

What If...

there was a thumb on each side of your hand?

_____
_____
_____
_____
_____
_____
_____
_____
_____
_____

we did not have fingerprints?

_____
_____
_____
_____
_____
_____
_____
_____
_____
_____

humans had no fingernails?

_____
_____
_____
_____
_____
_____
_____
_____
_____

there was an eye on the end of your index fingers?

_____
_____
_____
_____
_____
_____
_____

we used our fingerprints as identification and did not need signatures?

_____
_____
_____
_____
_____

Copyright © 1997 Gary Grimm & Associates

Careers in Science

Everyone knows what a pilot does. His job is to fly an airplane. It is a little more complicated than that. Every time a pilot begins a flight he becomes part scientist. He must be able to read and interpret several scientific instruments. He must know about weather, cloud formations, velocity, altitude, air pressure. This list could go on and on.

What aspects of science are involved in the day-to-day duties of the following professions?

Pharmacist _____
_____
_____

Geologist _____
_____
_____

Oceanographer _____
_____
_____

Anthropologist _____
_____
_____

Astronomer _____
_____
_____

Horticulturist _____
_____
_____

Nutritionist _____
_____
_____

Copyright © 1997 Gary Grimm & Associates

What Is a Scientist?

What does a scientist do? Try writing a one-sentence explanation.

_____

_____

Name some famous scientists. Try to think of ten. Briefly tell what each did.

Scientist	What He/She Did
_____	_____
_____	_____
_____	_____
_____	_____
_____	_____
_____	_____
_____	_____
_____	_____
_____	_____

Compare what you said each scientist did to your original definition. Do they match? Can you write a better sentence that answers the question, "What does a scientist do?"

_____

_____

_____

_____

_____

_____

_____

_____

                    Copyright © 1997 Gary Grimm & Associates

Sections
World
National
Local
Sports

Weather
High _____
Low _____
Wind _____

The Hometown Times

Science in the News!

Science isn't just in laboratories or classrooms. It is in the news every day, every week. Bring a copy of your local newspaper from home. Look through the newspaper and search for science-related topics and articles.

I found the following specific articles about science:

Although not the main issue of the article, science was involved in the following articles:

Pictures, graphs, diagrams relating to science were found in the following:

The most important science fact I learned from my newspaper search was

Copyright © 1997 Gary Grimm & Associates

Science in the Workplace

Many scientists work in laboratories. However, an archaeologist works at the site of an excavation, a conservationist works in the forest, and an oceanographer works near water. Science is everywhere. It is a part of many occupations. How is science a part of the following jobs?

Detective _____

_____

_____

Farmer _____

_____

_____

Beautician _____

_____

_____

Weatherman _____

_____

_____

Cook/Chef _____

_____

_____

Photographer _____

_____

_____

Animal Trainer _____

_____

_____

Copyright © 1997 Gary Grimm & Associates

Just Suppose

Just suppose all of our nourishment came from pills rather than from food.

Who would be out of a job?

_____
_____
_____
_____

How would a person's lifestyle change if all nourishment came from pills?

_____
_____
_____
_____

What businesses would fail?

_____
_____
_____

Would people be healthier or less healthy? Why?

_____
_____
_____
_____

Do you think that sometime in the future this might be possible? Why? Why not?

_____
_____
_____
_____

 Copyright © 1997 Gary Grimm & Associates

Let's Get Physical!

At the health club where you work, most of the participants are your age. Because you are a renowned physical fitness expert, you have designed a program of physical fitness for those who have a tendency to sit in front of a TV or play computer games for too many hours at a time.

When making your list of recommended activities, you kept in mind some things about these "couch potato" type people who will be participating in the program. These are

_____

_____

You have decided on the following list of games, exercises, and group activities that these people would probably enjoy.

Games	Exercises	Group Activities
_____	_____	_____
_____	_____	_____
_____	_____	_____
_____	_____	_____
_____	_____	_____
_____	_____	_____

Your goal for this group is_____

_____

In the space below, prepare a one-week schedule of the various forms of exercise you have designed. List how much time should be spent on each activity.

Sunday	**Monday**	**Tuesday**	**Wednesday**
Activity _____	Activity _____	Activity _____	Activity _____
_____	_____	_____	_____
Time _____	Time _____	Time _____	Time _____
Thursday	**Friday**	**Saturday**	**Notes**
Activity _____	Activity _____	Activity _____	_____
_____	_____	_____	_____
Time _____	Time _____	Time _____	_____

 Copyright © 1997 Gary Grimm & Associates

Trees! Trees! Trees!

There are approximately 20,000 kinds of trees on earth. More than 1000 kinds grow in the United States. Can you name 25 different trees? 50? 100? Give it a try. Take you list home and have your family members help you make your list grow.

Yes, a saguaro cactus is a tree!

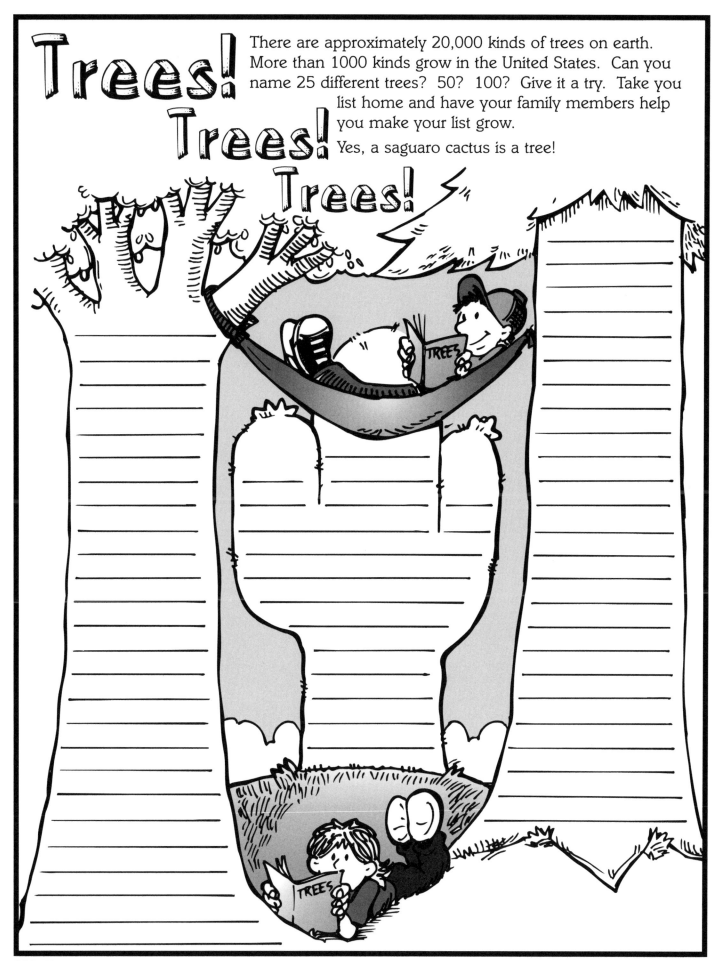

Copyright © 1997 Gary Grimm & Associates

Seasonal Thinking

How do you know it is spring, summer, fall, or winter? You may draw pictures or list signs of the seasons.

Spring

Summer

Fall

Winter

Copyright © 1997 Gary Grimm & Associates

Nature's Cleanup Committee

What do the following have in common?

☐ **Vultures** ☐ **Bacteria** ☐ **Maggots**

☐ **Rain** ☐ **Floods** ☐ **Fire**

☐ **Dung Beetles**

What would happen if dead animals were left right where they died? Think about all the different kinds of animals, their sizes, where they live. Think of all the kinds of problems it might cause for us. What might happen?

_____

_____

_____

Vultures, bacteria, and maggots (fly larvae) all help to take care of the problem, yet we often don't give them much respect.

When forest fires happen because lightning strikes dry trees or grasses, we often feel afraid because fires threaten our homes and possessions. However, fire is just another of nature's cleaning supplies. Think of some reasons why this is true.

_____

_____

Rain and floods also help in the cleanup process, benefitting both nature and humankind. Pretend you are rain or a stream or river that is overflowing its banks. Write your thoughts about how you're helping the environment.

_____

_____

How does wind contribute to this cleaning process?

_____

_____

Copyright © 1997 Gary Grimm & Associates

What Do Trees Supply?

What do trees provide? List products and benefits from A to Z.

A _____

_____

B _____

_____

C _cardboard, cork, cherries_____

_____

D _____

_____

E _____

_____

F _____

_____

G _____

_____

H _homes_____

_____

I _____

_____

J _____

_____

K _____

_____

L _____

_____

M _____

N _____

_____

O _____

_____

P _____

_____

Q _____

R _____

_____

S _shelter_____

_____

T _____

_____

U _____

_____

V _____

_____

W _____

_____

XYZ _____

Copyright © 1997 Gary Grimm & Associates

"Good Morning, Sunshine"

I'm busy even when it's cloudy

The sun is more important to man than any other object in the sky. All life on earth (man, plants, animals) depends on the sun for survival. The sun is very dependable. It rises every day and it sets every day. It never fails to perform its duty.

What does the sun do all day? List below things the sun does.

1. _it warms things up like the air, a sidewalk, and animals_
2. _____
3. _____
4. _____
5. _____
6. _____
7. _____
8. _____
9. _____
10. _____

What if the sun stopped shining? What are some of the things that would happen?

1. _____
2. _____
3. _____
4. _____
5. _tanning salons would prosper_
6. _____
7. _____
8. _____
9. _____
10. _____

Copyright © 1997 Gary Grimm & Associates

Happy Trails

START

There are many neat things in nature to learn . . . many right in your neighborhood or hometown.

Your school has been asked to create a nature trail in your community, a trail where people from other parts of the United States can walk and learn about the trees, wildflowers, birds, insects, animals and other things just by walking along and reading the signs and observing.

Where would this trail go in your neighborhood or community?

_____

_____

_____

What birds would there be to hear and possibly see?

_____

_____

_____

What trees could be identified and labeled?

_____

_____

_____

List wildflowers that may be found in your area.

_____

_____

What animals live in your area?

_____

_____

_____

On a separate sheet of paper draw a map of the area you have chosen. Create a trail and name it. Identify what there would be to see, hear, feel, smell.

     Copyright © 1997 Gary Grimm & Associates

Answers from Eco-Man

Eco-man is the Dear Abby of ecology and conservation. He is a world-renowned resource on our natural resources. Three of his readers have written him letters. Pretend you are Eco-man and respond with a letter of sound advice.

Dear Eco-man

I own a grocery store. I want to be ecology-minded. There are paper sacks, plastic bags, cardboard cartons, spoiled fruit and vegetables every day. What can I do to save resources?

Barney from Boston

_____
_____
_____
_____
_____
_____
_____
_____
_____
_____

Dear Eco-man

We just studied about ecology in school. Our teacher wants each of us to do what we can to help clean our environment. I live on the 26th floor of an apartment building in the middle of New York City. What are three things I can do?

Hannah Highrise

_____
_____
_____
_____
_____
_____
_____
_____
_____
_____

Dear Eco-man

My mother insists on using plastic tableware, paper plates, napkins, etc. If it is paper or plastic, she uses it. I don't think we own real dishes. I know that using real dishes and silverware would conserve resources. What can I say to my mother to get her to change?

Darling Daughter

_____
_____
_____
_____
_____
_____
_____

Copyright © 1997 Gary Grimm & Associates

It's Not Easy to Say NO!

A picnic is great fun. It's food, fun, family and friends. It's also paper and plastic. Among the ants you can find paper napkins, plastic utensils, paper plates, plastic wrap, paper sacks, plastic cups and . . . mountains of paper and plastic. It is convenient and practical to use all that paper and plastic. But what a nightmare for the trees living nearby to see what has happened to their cousins.

Perhaps paper and plastic are acceptable at a picnic; but some families use it every day, maybe even three times a day. What a waste! Just think of the space needed in a landfill to put 1,000,000 plastic knives, forks, and spoons each day.

But the problem is not that easy to solve. Answer the following questions and see why. If paper and plastic tableware (napkins, glasses, plates, and silverware) were banned, who would lose their jobs?

_____

_____

How would this affect the fast-food businesses? _____

_____

_____

What other businesses would be affected? _____

_____

_____

What can be done to control the amount of paper and plastic used in the food industry?

_____

_____

_____

What is your opinion? Should paper and plastic be eliminated from the table? Why? Why not?

_____

_____

_____

_____

Earth-Friendly Deeds

You can earn five GOOD DEED ribbons. Most of the time when we think about doing good deeds we think about doing them for people. We help our neighbors and friends. But we can do good deeds for the earth. Every day there are many things we can do to make the earth a cleaner, better place. Draw a picture or write your idea in each circle. What is a good deed you can do for the air, energy, plants, animals and our water supply?

TORNADO · **CHINOOK** · **HURRICANE** · **TRADE WINDS** · **ALBERTA CLIPPER** · **BREEZE** · **GALE**

ZEPHYR · **TYPHOON** · **PREVAILING WIND** · **MISTRAL** · **WHIRLWIND** · **WINDCHILL** · **MONSOONS**

DOLDRUMS · **WIND TUNNEL** · **STORM**

Blowing in the Wind

We take so many aspects of the weather for granted. One of those weather conditions that gets little of our attention is the wind. Gusts of air we call "wind" affect us and our lives and the lives of others every day. But we seldom think about the wind unless it becomes strong.

How does the wind, or the lack of it, affect . . .

the weather _____

_____

_____

farming _____

_____

_____

sounds and noises _____

_____

_____

outdoor sports _____

_____

_____

transportation _____

_____

_____

When is the wind a friend? _____

_____

_____

_____

When is the wind an enemy? _____

_____

_____

_____

All the terms that form the border are related to wind. Can you identify these terms? Use the reverse side of the activity sheet.

Copyright © 1997 Gary Grimm & Associates

The ABCs of "Mammaldom"

A mammal is an animal with hair and mammary glands on its body. The word mammal comes from the Latin word *mamma* which means "breast." Mammals have breasts and the females of the species feed milk that is produced in the breasts to their young. Birds, fish, snakes, and insects are not mammals because they do not have these characteristics. Can you name a mammal (or mammals) for each letter of the alphabet?

A _____   N _____
B _____   O _____
C _____   P _____
D _____   Q _____
E _____   R _____
F _____   S _____
G _____   T _____
H _____   U _____
I _____   V _____
J _____   W _____
K _____   X _____
L _____   Y _____
M _____   Z _____

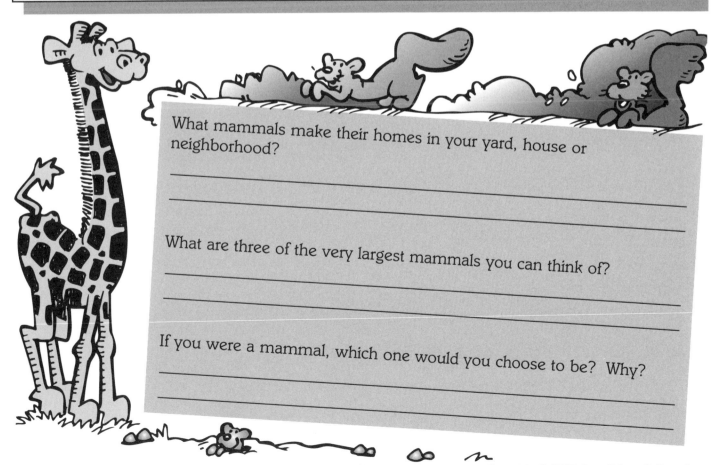

What mammals make their homes in your yard, house or neighborhood?

_____
_____

What are three of the very largest mammals you can think of?

_____
_____

If you were a mammal, which one would you choose to be? Why?

_____
_____

                          Copyright © 1997 Gary Grimm & Associates

This Is for the Birds

TIME YOURSELF! List as many birds as you can in three minutes. Use the lines to the right.

READY! SET! GO!

Really think!

DON'T BE A BIRDBRAIN!

Did you get at least twenty? See if you can add more birds doing the following. (You will think of so many that you will probably have to use the backside of this paper.)

1. Think about the birds you see around a bird feeder or in your yard.

2. How about birds that sports teams are named after?

3. Which ones have colors in the names or are especially colorful?

4. Have you ever been to an aviary at a zoo?

5. Don't forget pet birds.

6. How about those flightless birds?

7. Then, there are birds of prey.

8. Some people really enjoy watching water birds.

9. Some birds are hunted or appear on the table as foods.

10. Go ahead. Add fictitious birds. "Big Bird" would love it.

Do you know me?

Count them.

My grand total is _____.

On the back, list what the purposes of birds are.

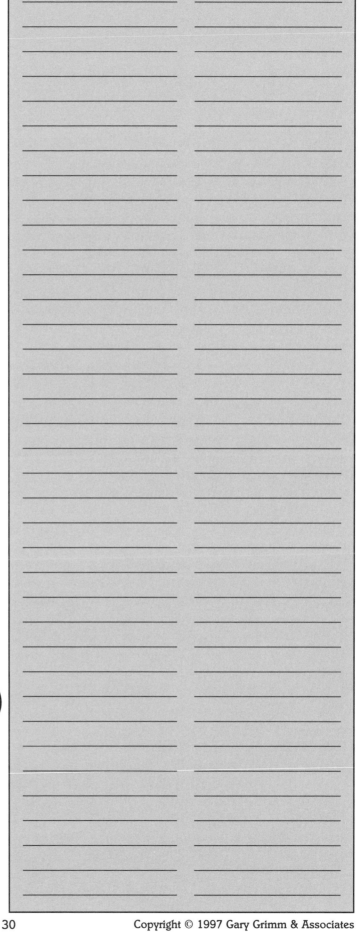

Copyright © 1997 Gary Grimm & Associates

Is It Animal, Vegetable, or Mineral?

It's easy to name twenty-five animals. Vegetables are also easy. Minerals are more difficult. Everything is either animal, vegetable, or mineral. Corn growing in a field is a vegetable. Gasoline for a car is mineral. Yes, it is fairly easy to determine to which kingdom an item belongs.

Below you will find listed some small words. To which kingdom does each item belong? Circle the members of the animal kingdom. "X" out the minerals and draw a box around the words that belong to the vegetable kingdom. You will most likely need to have a dictionary handy.

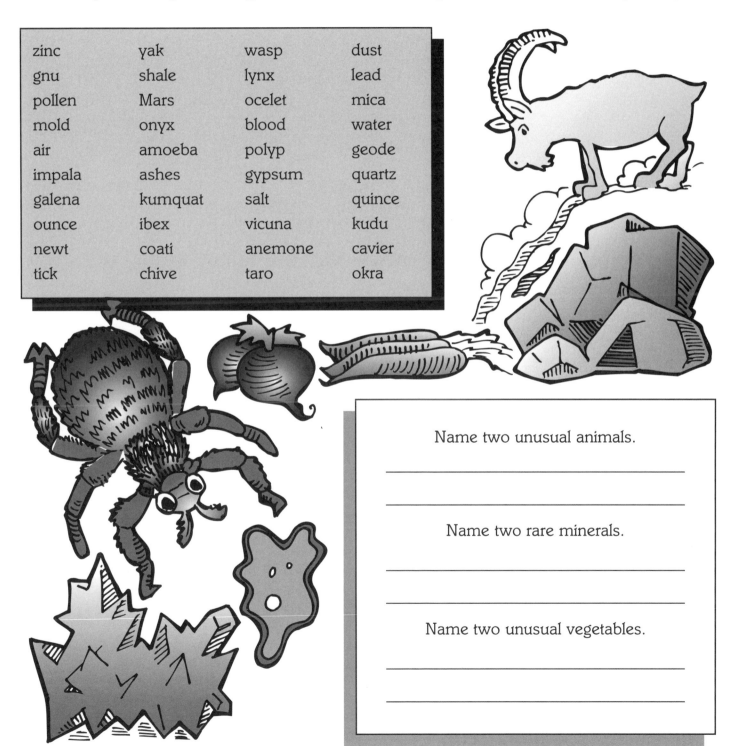

zinc	yak	wasp	dust
gnu	shale	lynx	lead
pollen	Mars	ocelet	mica
mold	onyx	blood	water
air	amoeba	polyp	geode
impala	ashes	gypsum	quartz
galena	kumquat	salt	quince
ounce	ibex	vicuna	kudu
newt	coati	anemone	cavier
tick	chive	taro	okra

Name two unusual animals.

_____

_____

Name two rare minerals.

_____

_____

Name two unusual vegetables.

_____

_____

Copyright © 1997 Gary Grimm & Associates

Domesticated or Wild?

Some animals are wild; others are domesticated.

What is the difference between a domesticated animal and a wild animal? _____

_____

Can you think of a synonym for *domesticated*? _____

Why has man domesticated some animals? _____

What do animals provide man? Food, of course, but what else?

Animal	What It Provides
_____	_____
_____	_____
_____	_____
_____	_____
_____	_____
_____	_____
_____	_____

Continue your list on the back.

What animal do you think would be beneficial for man to domesticate? Why?

_____

_____

Don't Bug Me!

Insects sometimes get their names from the way they look. The praying mantis and the walking stick are two examples. Draw a picture of what any three of the listed insects could look like if you pictured them exactly like their names.

cornborer
grasshopper
daddy longlegs
bedbug
lightning bug
dragonfly
horsefly
carpenter ant

On the back of this paper, design an insect that does not exist. Give it a name and a form. Let your imagination be free!

Copyright © 1997 Gary Grimm & Associates

It's All in the Family

Hi, Mom! Hi, Dad! That is what many of us humans call our parents. The adult human female is called a mother and the male is called a father. The young is called a child (children). Try matching the male/female and young name of the following animals.

Male	Female		Animal		Young
A. Buck	Doe	____	Bear	____	A. Fawn
B. Cob	Pen	____	Goose	____	B. Kid
C. Ram	Ewe	____	Deer	____	C. Gosling
D. Billy	Nanny	____	Swan	____	D. Cygnet
E. Dog	Vixen	**C**	Sheep	**H**	E. Calf
F. He-Bear	She-bear	____	Goat	____	F. Cub
G. Gander	Goose	____	Whale	____	G. Kit
H. Bull	Cow	____	Swine	____	H. Lamb
I. Boar	Sow	____	Fox	____	I. Duckling
J. Drake	Hen	____	Duck	____	J. Piglet

Can you think of a couple of others?

_____

_____

_____

If you are not already in a playful mood, relax and let your mind play. Make up some male, female, and names of young for the following animals. Don't worry about the authentic names. You may look those up later.

Animal	Male	Female	Young
Leopard	_____	_____	_____
Alligator	_____	_____	_____
Porcupine	_____	_____	_____

Now try these make-believe animals.

Dragon	_____	_____	_____
Unicorn	_____	_____	_____
Girtle*	_____	_____	_____
Elerilla**	_____	_____	_____

* A girtle is half giraffe and half turtle.

** You can guess what an elerilla is.

 Copyright © 1997 Gary Grimm & Associates

Something Old, Something New

Listed below are some common everyday items. Did they exist when your parents were your age? Did they exist when your grandparents were your age? Take a guess. Write Y for "yes, they existed then" or N for "no they did not exist." Take this activity home and get some expert advice from those who know.

Item	Parent	Grandparent
television		
JELL-O™		
microwave oven		
frozen pizza		
the Internet		
CD players		
in-line skates		
Tylenol™/Nuprin™		
video games		
contact lens		
Scotch™ Tape		
candy bars		
ATM machines		
Self-service gas		

Now list twenty more things that you think did not exist when your grandparents were your age.

_____

_____

_____

_____

_____

_____

     Copyright © 1997 Gary Grimm & Associates

It Takes 100 Inventions to Get Dressed

For you to be looking at this piece of paper and reading this sentence, there had to be several inventions.

a. copy machine so the teacher could make copies
b. electricity so the copy machine would work
c. printing press to print the original copy
d. ink to print the words and letters
e. alphabet so the words could be created
f. saw to cut down the tree that provided the paper

Now think about what you are wearing. List everything that you have on – items of clothing, a belt with a buckle, jewelry, nail polish, deodorant. List everything.

_____

_____

_____

Now list some of the inventions that were needed so that you can be dressed the way you are.

a. _____

b. _____

c. _____

d. _____

e. _____

f. _____

g. _____

h. _____

i. _____

j. _____

k. _____

l. _____

m. _____

n. _____

Continue on the back of this paper.

The Future Begins ... Today ... Right Now!

What will be next? Inventions are made each and every day. Things happen fast. Someone invents something and shortly someone else has improved the original or invented something better. Here is your chance. Put on your thinking cap and invent/create something for the following areas. You may draw and label or just explain.

Transportation
Land/Water

City/Country

Personal/Group

Communications
With Friends

Long Distance

Entertainment

Health Care
Diagnosis

Treatment

Calling 249*%T/8

What if when you were born, a tiny computer chip had been placed in your inner ear. This chip would allow your parents and, as you grew older, your teachers, the police, or anyone to keep track of you if you were in danger or to find you if you were lost or kidnapped. The chip would be able to send and receive radio messages. Just think about it. Even pets could receive chips so their owners could keep track of them. A lost puppy could be returned to its home immediately. A chip like this will probably be possible in just a few years.

What are some of the good and not-so-good things that might happen if such devices were available to the mass market?

_____

_____

_____

_____

Some laws might have to be enacted to protect people who are wearing the chips. What are three laws that would protect the wearer?

1. _____

_____

2. _____

_____

3. _____

_____

Just as soon as something is invented there are additional inventions that improve the original invention. How might you improve the original chip?

_____

_____

How might this device help car drivers, pilots, people in the military, the elderly, people on vacation, children, people who are ill? Continue your answer on the back.

_____

_____

_____

Copyright © 1997 Gary Grimm & Associates

SPACE

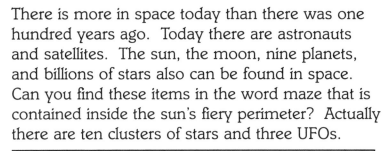

There is more in space today than there was one hundred years ago. Today there are astronauts and satellites. The sun, the moon, nine planets, and billions of stars also can be found in space. Can you find these items in the word maze that is contained inside the sun's fiery perimeter? Actually there are ten clusters of stars and three UFOs.

Word Bank		
Stars (10)	Sun	Satellite
Moon	UFOs (3)	Pluto
Neptune	Uranus	Saturn
Earth	Jupiter	Mars
Venus	Mercury	Astronaut
(Twenty-six words in all)		

Can you identify the planets as well as their order according to the distances from the sun? Print the name of each planet on the appropriate blank.

Billions of dollars have been spent on space exploration. Do you think the findings have been worth the dollars spent? Do you think with all the problems that exist on earth the money has been wisely spent? What else do we need to know about space? Why do we need to know about space? What is your opinion about space exploration? Write your thoughts on the reverse side.

```
          V E F S J U S
        J S E S T A R S F T
        U P N E P T U N E O A
      S P A U U L E S T A R S R
      U I M S F U L A S T A R S S
      X T E A O T L C R R M U T T
      M E R S S O I R M T A R A A
      A R C T R S T Y O J H T R R
      R U U R A Z E D O S S H S S
      S F R O T Y S U N R T R S T
      V O Y N S T A R S A A E A
        S S A T U R N V T R V
        M U R A N U S S S
          T S R A T S K
```

Copyright © 1997 Gary Grimm & Associates

A-mazing Teeth

Can you find the way through the maze so the toothbrush can find the tooth? Along the way you will find some scrambled words associated with dentistry and tooth care. Unscramble each word you encounter along the route. WRITE the word in the appropriate blanks below. Finally, unscramble any remaining words and PRINT those words in the appropriate blanks.

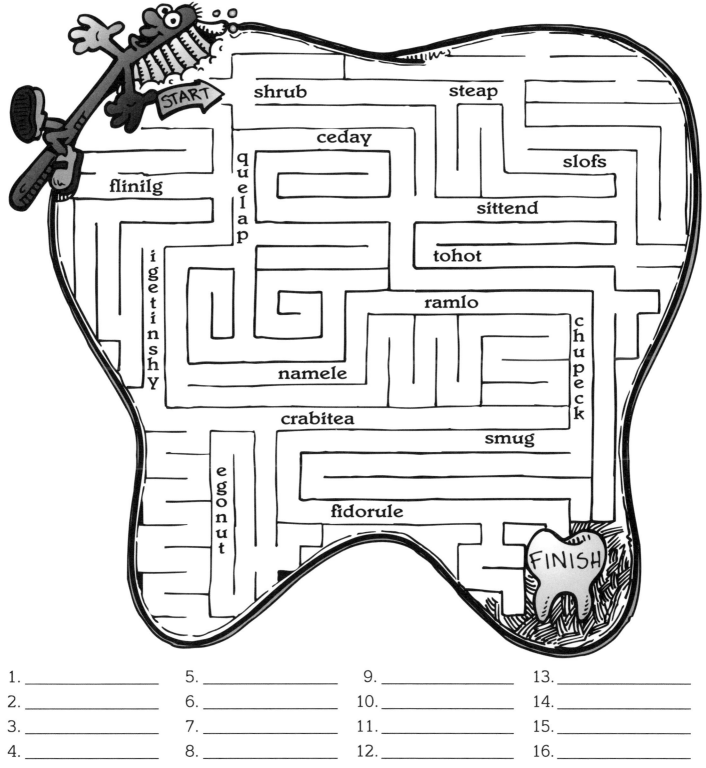

1. _____   5. _____   9. _____   13. _____

2. _____   6. _____   10. _____   14. _____

3. _____   7. _____   11. _____   15. _____

4. _____   8. _____   12. _____   16. _____

Now on the back of this paper, use the unscrambled words in sentences. You may use more than one word in a sentence.

GGA113   40   Copyright © 1997 Gary Grimm & Associates